LEVEL 3

Published in Moonstone
by Rupa Publications India Pvt. Ltd 2022
7/16, Ansari Road, Daryaganj
New Delhi 110002

Sales centres:
Allahabad Bengaluru Chennai
Hyderabad Jaipur Kathmandu
Kolkata Mumbai

Copyright © Rupa Publications India Pvt. Ltd 2022

The views and opinions expressed in this book are
the authors' own and the facts are as reported by them
which have been verified to the extent possible,
and the publishers are not in any way liable for the same.

All rights reserved.
No part of this publication may be reproduced, transmitted,
or stored in a retrieval system, in any form or by any means,
electronic, mechanical, photocopying, recording or otherwise,
without the prior permission of the publisher.

P-ISBN: 978-93-5520-642-8
E-ISBN: 978-93-5520-643-5

First impression 2022

10 9 8 7 6 5 4 3 2 1

The moral right of the authors has been asserted.

Printed in India
This book is sold subject to the condition that it shall not,
by way of trade or otherwise, be lent, resold, hired out, or otherwise
circulated, without the publisher's prior consent, in any form of binding
or cover other than that in which it is published.

Contents

Let's Recap 4

Digraph Ch 6

Digraph Sh 8

Consonant Blend Br. 10

Consonant Blend Cr. 12

Digraph Th 14

Digraph Wh 16

Learn More 18

Consonant Blend Dr 22

Consonant Blend Fr. 24

Consonant Blend Gr. 26

Consonant Blend Tr. 28

Consonant Blend Pr. 30

Learn More 32

Consonant Blend Bl 36

Consonant Blend Cl 38

Consonant Blend Fl 40

Consonant Blend Gl 42

Consonant Blend Pl 44

Learn More 46

Short or Long Vowel? 47

Long Vowel A 48

Let's Recap

Look at the objects and write their names.

Look at the picture clues. Complete the sentences by filling in the missing words.

1. Tom had a _____ .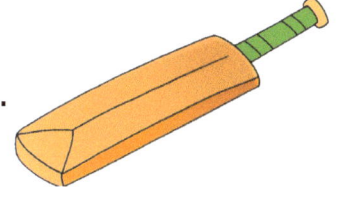

2. Sam had a _____ .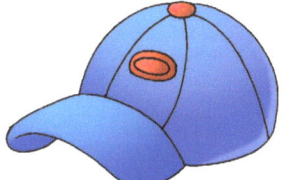

3. The _____ had a nap.

4. A pan and a _____ .

5. Dad has a _____ .

6. Please ring the _____ .

7. Open the _____ .

8. John found a _____ .

Digraph Ch

Read these words aloud. Can you hear the ch sound?

Chick

Child

Beach

Pitch

Witch

Circle the ch sound in the poem.

Chuck the Chicken!

Crunchy chocolates

Yummy cheese

And ketchup

In the kitchen

O what a treat it is,

For Chuck the chicken!

Teaching Tips:
Make the students chant the poem with a rhythm to practice the ch sound.

Add ch to complete the words and then read them aloud.

| ……alk | ……ew | Mun…… | ……ild |

| In…… | Bea…… | Pun…… | ……in |

| ……eese | Lun…… | Brun…… | ……eek |

| ……op | Tea…… | ……illi | ……ain |

| ……ips | ……urch | Bun…… | ……ocolate |

Digraph Sh

Read these words aloud. Can you hear the sh sound?

Shed

Shell

Splash

Ash

Shoot

Read the story. Circle the words with sh sound.

Shelly went with her mother to shop. Shelly wanted a new shirt and a pair of new shoes. Her mother wanted some sugar, shampoo and fish.

Shelly found a pink shirt. She also found a pair of shiny shoes.

Shelly had a great day.

Teaching Tips:
Place a finger on your lips to indicate the sh sound.

Read the words.

Ash Bash   Cash Shock   Hush Brush

Sheep Shut   Shook Sheet   Dish Shift

Shin Shelf   Wish Fish   Rush Ship

Look at the pictures. Can you find the names of these objects in the word search below?

Ship

Shirt

s	h	a	r	k	s	t
k	s	h	s	o	h	r
s	h	t	h	s	e	m
h	o	d	i	j	l	v
i	e	a	p	n	l	r
r	s	l	c	y	x	o
t	i	m	j	w	i	l

Shark

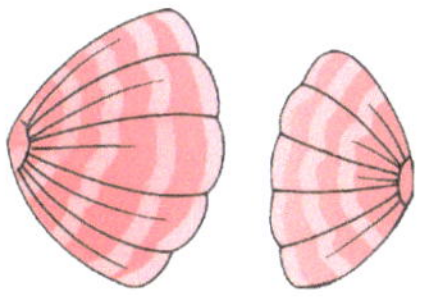

Shell

Shoe

9

Consonant Blend Br

Read the words aloud. Underline the br sound in every word.

The words begin with the .... sound.

Teaching Tips:

Use the following story. B is a friendly letter. It likes to sit with the other letters in his classroom. When it sits next to the letter R, the B says 'buh' and the R says 'rrr' and together they shout 'bruh'. Let children say 'bruh'. A similar story can also be used to teach the blends, cr, dr, fr and gr.

Look at the words below. Now pick the ones that begin with br and write each on the brick wall.

Brick	Bread	Brass	Brain	Brother	Brave
Fry	Try	Brown	Dry	Broom	Hair
Cry	Brain	Bride	Chair	Bright	Brush

Consonant Blend Cr

Read these words aloud. Can you hear the cr sound?

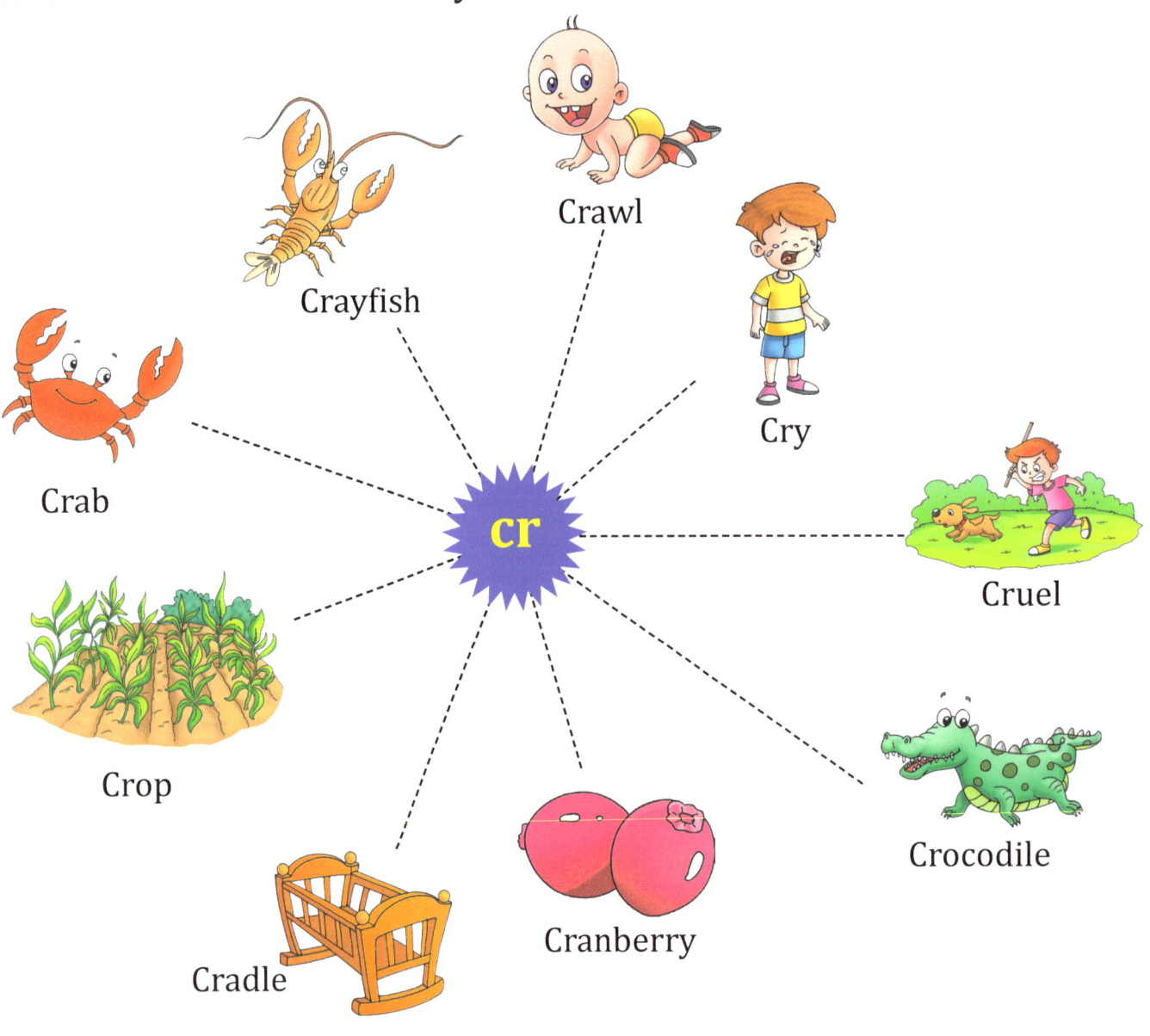

The words begin with the .... sound.

Teaching Tips:
Instruct the students to read words that contain consonant blends by saying the sounds of the two consonants and the other parts of the words quickly, one right after the other.

Look at the pictures. Can you find the names of these objects in the word search below?

Crab

Crow

Crown

Craft

l	c	r	a	f	t	w
c	r	a	c	k	m	c
o	c	r	a	y	o	n
c	r	o	w	s	u	w
w	h	w	q	t	v	t
w	c	r	o	w	n	x
x	c	r	a	b	n	l

Crack

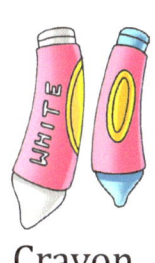
Crayon

Complete the words by filling in the missing letters.

........ane	........ispy	........oss
........eek	........ib	........ate

13

Digraph Th

Theo

Theo is thin

Theo has a long chin

Theo has yellow teeth

Theo lives in a hole

Because he is a mole.

Read the words aloud.

Set 1

Thank   Thing   Thrust

Set 2

Than   Them   This

Can you hear the difference between the sound th in both the sets of words?

Teaching Tips:

1) Soft th: this sound is 'voiced.' It vibrates a little bit. It is mostly used in common words, and the tongue is in the same position as hard th. 2) Hard th: this sound is not 'voiced.' It is made by putting the tongue between or just behind the teeth. The tongue presses and then moves away. The tongue is thickly pressed for a moment–the sound should not be the same as D.

Read the words aloud. Circle the th sound in each word.

This	These	The
Those	Thumb	Smooth
That	Cloth	Thump
Teeth	There	Moth
Thank	Them	Froth

Digraph Wh

Whitney and the Whale

Who saw the whale?

Whitney saw the whale.

Where did Whitney see the whale?

Whitney saw it near the wharf.

What was the whale like?

Whitney said it had whiskers

It was white,

And it whistled.

Choose the correct word to complete the sentences.

| Why | whale | Who | wheel | white |

1. .... is the person next to you?
2. Use the steering .... to turn the car.
3. .... are you late?
4. Have you seen a .... leopard?
5. The blue .... is the largest animal on earth.

Teaching Tips:

Pass a bowl with chits around the class. Each chit should have one word with the *wh* sound. Ask each child to pick a chit and pronounce the word.

Read the words aloud. Circle the words with the wh sound.

Whale

Walk

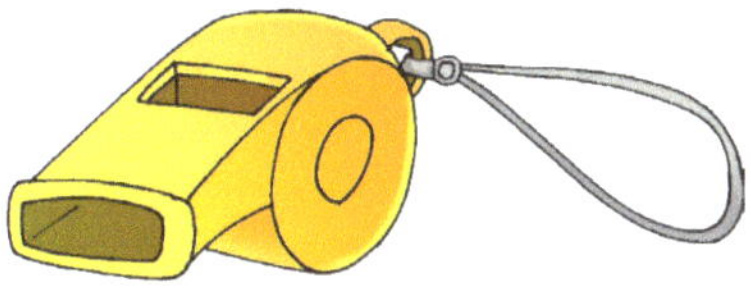

Whistle

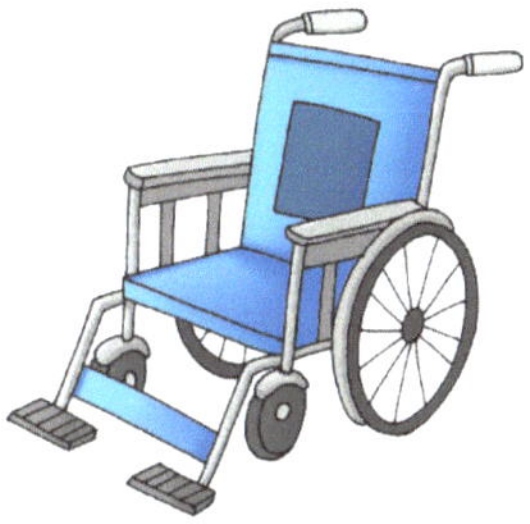

Wheelchair

Wheelbarrow

Wolf

wh

Window

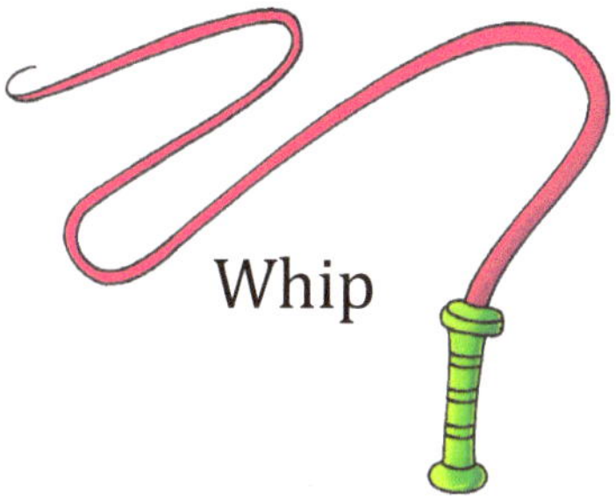

Whip

White

Wharf

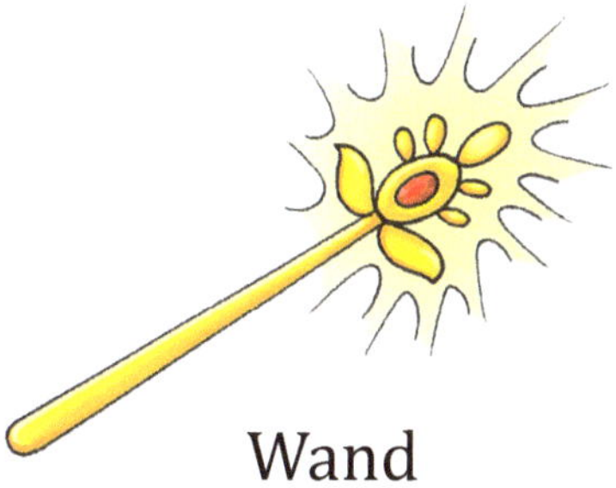

Wand

Winter

Learn More

A. **Guess the sh and ch words below with the given hints.**

1. You sit on it. ....

2. It is below your mouth. ....

3. You find it on the beach. ....

4. It is used to wash your hair. ....

5. You can write with it on the board. ....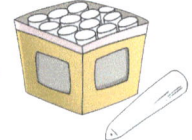

6. People go and pray in it. ....

B. **Write the words for the picture.**

1. The .... is green.

2. This is number ....

3. The .... is on the hill.

4. The .... of the bus goes round and round.

5. I pricked my ....

6. This is a ....

C. Name the object in each picture and listen to its beginning sound. Write the sound on the line below.

Sh   Th   Ch   Wh

....

....

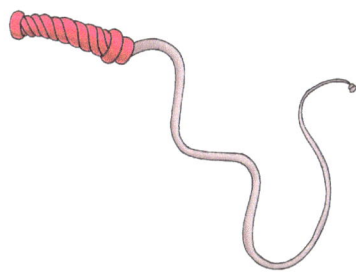

....

D. Fill in the missing sounds to complete the words.

..... ew   ..... ink   ..... ips

..... eel   ..... ush   ..... ree

..... eep   ..... ip   ..... ake

..... umb   Lun .....   Fa ..... er

E. **Look at the pictures and write the words in the box underneath the picture the words may start or end with sh, ch or th. The first one has been done as an example.**

Ship		
Chain	Bath	Wish
Shells	Sheep	Cheese
Shirt	Path	Shelf

Consonant Blend Dr

Read these words aloud. Colour the blend dr in each word.

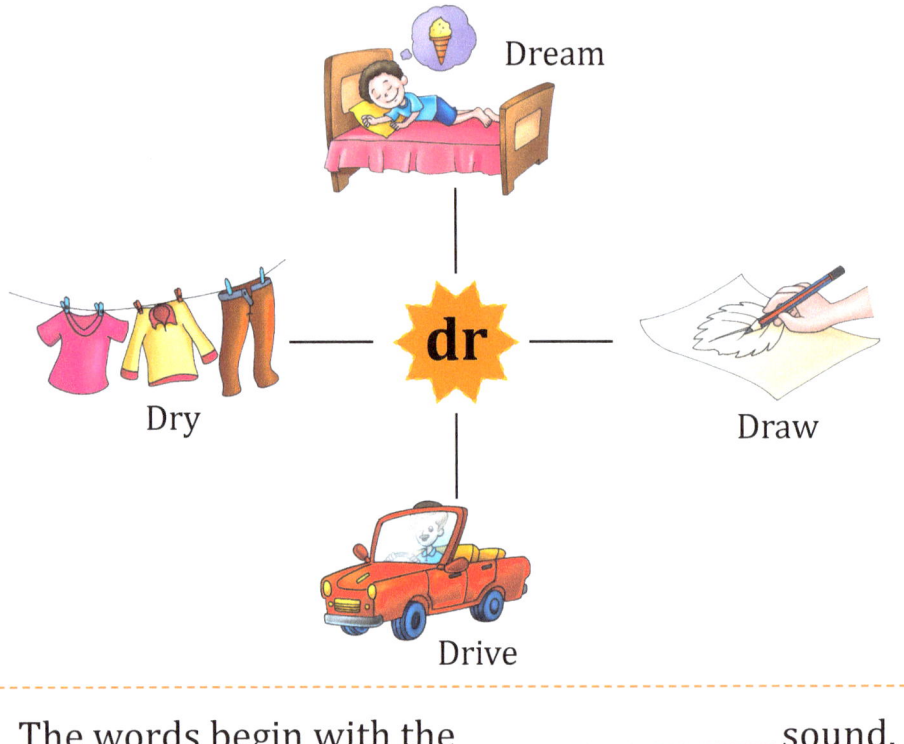

The words begin with the .... sound.

Read and underline the dr words in the poem.

Draco's Dream

Draco the dragon had a dream.
Draco dreamed that he drove a car,
And went to the city that was far.
Draco bought a drink and a dress,
He draped the dress around his waist,
Sipped the drink and drove back in haste.

Teaching Tips:
Ask the children to say a few words that have the dr sound in them.

Read aloud the words. Underline the blend dr in each word.

Consonant Blend Fr

Read these words aloud. Colour the blend fr in each word.

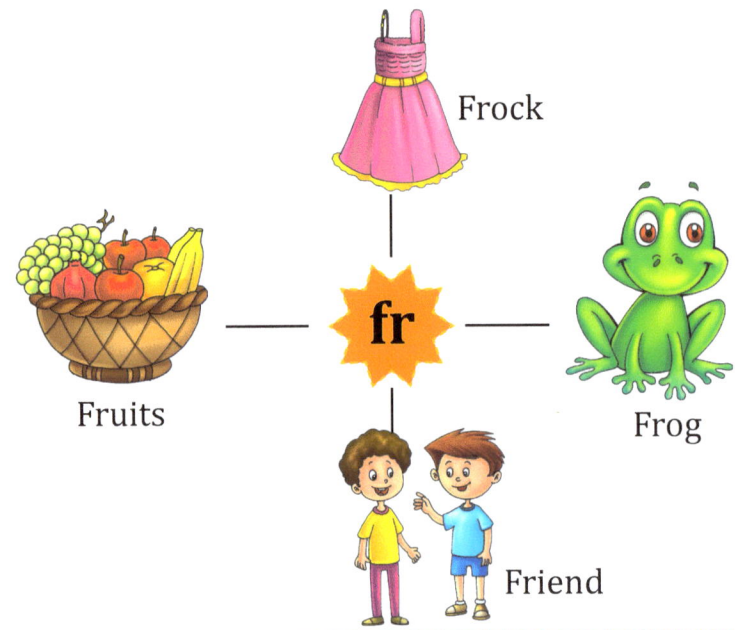

The words begin with the .... sound.

Read and underline the fr words in the poem.

Forgetful Fred

Forgetful Fred
Went to the shop,
There he forgot
The baby's frock,
And the playing block.
He forgot the fresh fruit,
And the boot.
'Why am I so forgetful?' Fred thought,
And asked the doctor to give him a shot.

Teaching Tips:
Ask the children to breakup the fr sound from the words in the poem. For example, break Fred into Fr + ed.

Look at the pictures and solve the crosswords. You can take the help of the words given below.

Frock   Fruits   Frame   Friend   Freeze   Fry   Fries   Frail

Consonant Blend Gr

Read these words aloud. Colour the blend gr in each word.

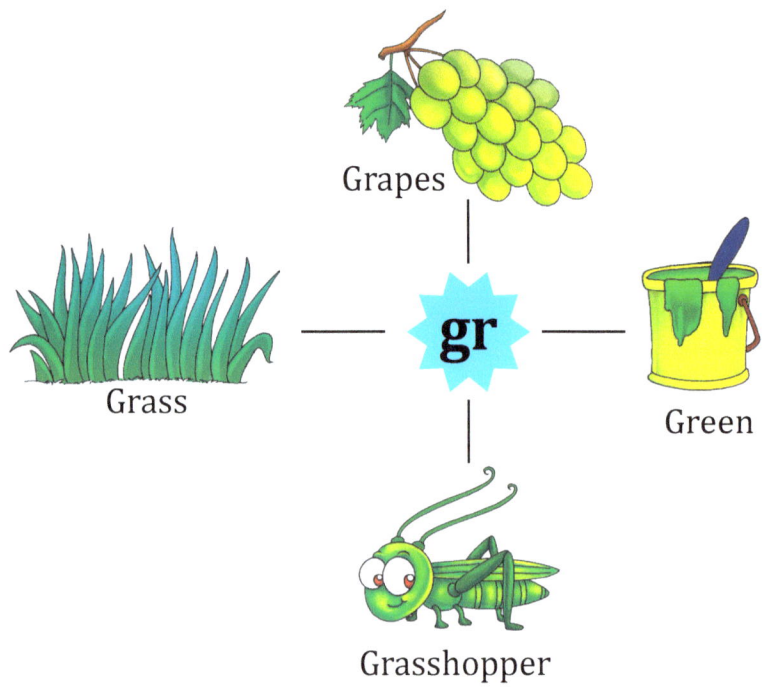

Circle the gr words in the poem.

Grace's Family

Grace went to Greece

To meet Gretel, her niece.

Grace and Gretel went to Greenland,

To meet Gretel's Grandfather.

Grandfather took them to Grandmother,

At last Grace's family was together.

Teaching Tips:

Fill a bag with small objects or pictures. Show them to the students and ask them to name the object. Ask them if the names have the gr sound in them or not.

Look at the pictures. Read the names. Now find these words in the word search below.

grill

gravel

grave

greet

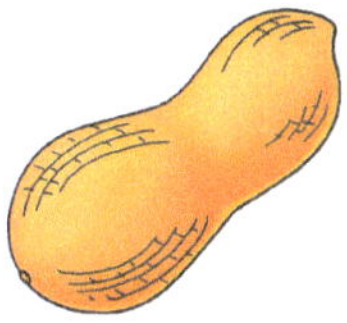

groundnut

grater

h	s	g	b	g	g	g	g	g
i	g	r	e	r	r	r	r	r
g	o	o	g	i	a	a	o	a
r	q	u	r	z	n	n	c	v
a	w	n	a	z	d	d	e	e
v	v	d	t	l	p	m	r	l
e	w	n	e	y	a	a	r	c
g	x	u	r	g	r	e	e	t
r	d	t	p	g	r	i	l	l

grandpa

grocer

grizzly

grandma

27

Consonant Blend Tr

Read these words aloud. Colour the blend tr in each word.

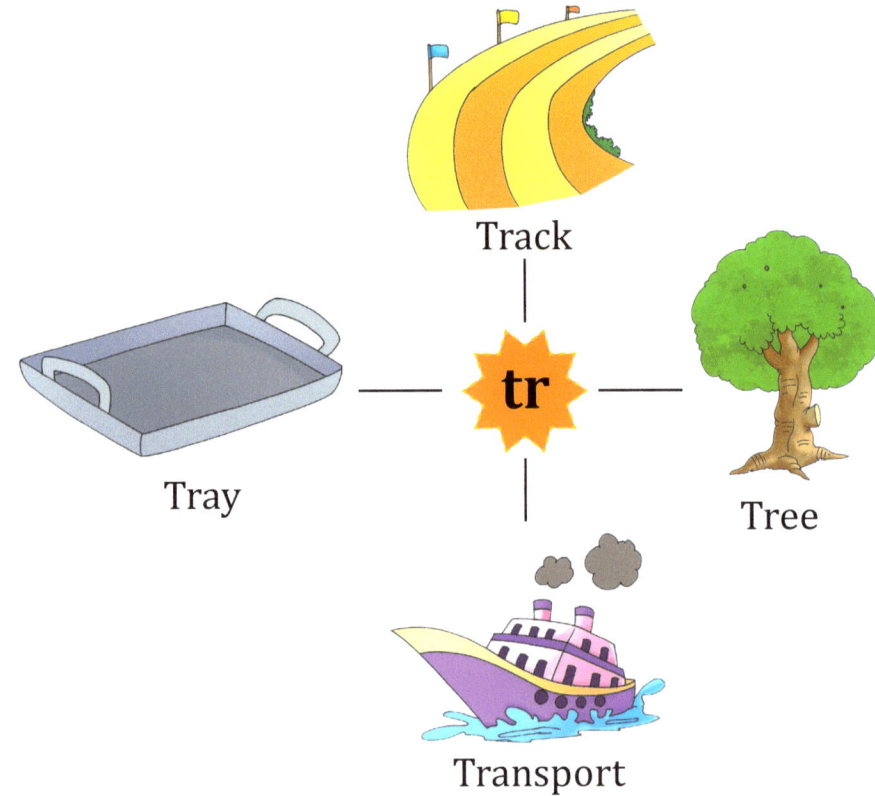

Circle the tr words in the poem.

Trick or Treat

Troy sat in his trolley

With Holly, Polly and Molly

Trab and Travis pushed the trolley

They all sang 'Tra-la-la-la-la'

They knocked on every door

And screamed, 'Trick or Treat?'

Some said treat, some said tricks

Oh the Halloween night was truly fun!

Blend it.

Tr + ain = ⬜

Tr + ay = ⬜

Tr + ip = ⬜

Tr + ap = ⬜

Tr + actor = ⬜

Tr + affic = ⬜

Write the names of three means of transport starting with tr.

.... , ... and ....

Consonant Blend Pr

Read the words aloud. Can you hear the pr sound?

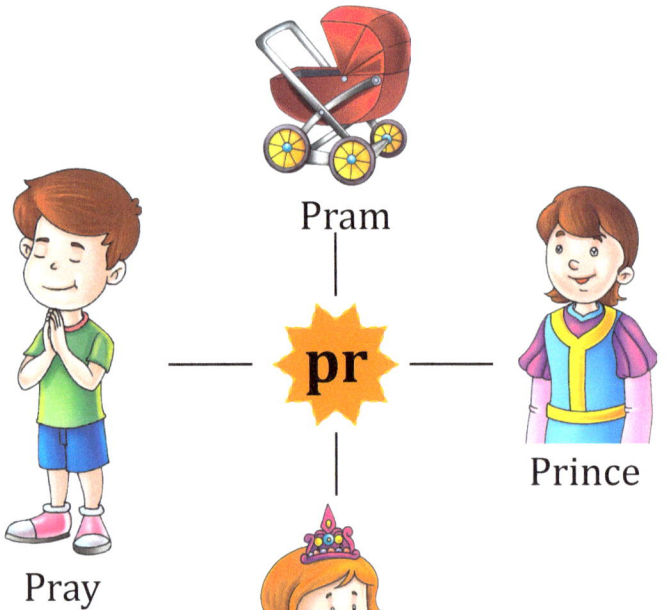

Read the story and circle the pr words.

Priya got a pet dog. She called him Present. Present and Priya played all day. Priya was proud of Present. She praised him a lot. Priya prayed and thanked God for her precious pet. She promised to love Present with all her heart.

Teaching Tips:
Ask the children to make up a story with a princess and prince as characters.

Fill in the blanks with the correct pr word from the list below.

| prize | press | prawn | pretzels | praying mantis | priest |

1. Joey had a ....  for dinner.

2. Tina saw a ....  in the garden.

3. Do you like to eat ....  ?

4. Do not ....  the bell.

5. Father John is a ....  .

6. I won the first ....  .

Learn More

A. **Choose the correct word from the word bank to answer the following questions.**

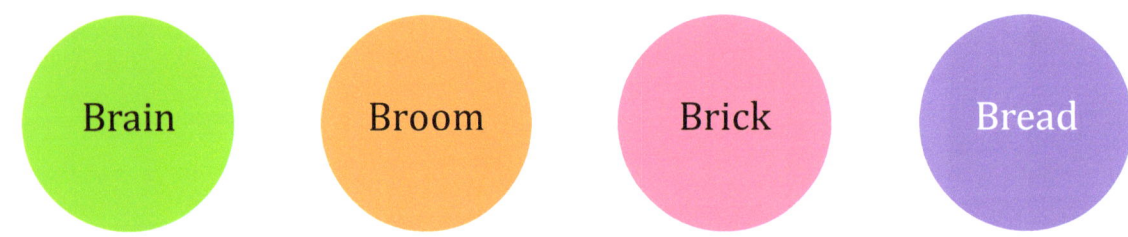

1. You use it to sweep. ....

2. It is a part of your body. ....

3. We eat it with jam. ....

4. This is used to build a house. ....

B. **Look at the picture. Say the word. Write the beginning blend in the box.**

....

....

....

....

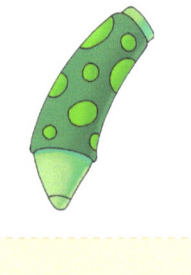
....

....

C. **Colour the words that begin with gr blue. Colour the words that begin with pr green. Colour the words that begin with cr red.**

| Grasshopper | Grass | Grapefruit |

| Grand | Grandchild | Pray |

| Pram | Princess | Prick |

| Crab | Cry | Creep |

| Crazy | Crawl |

D. Look at the pictures. Write the correct beginning consonant blend from the list below in the blank to spell the word.

| Br | Cr | Tr | Dr | Fr | Gr | Pr |

Br occoli

Tr ophy

Cr ib

Pr incess

Cr ab

Dr agonfly

Tr am

Tr actor

Fr own

Fr uit

Cr ayon

Pr oud

34

E. Story time

Read the story and underline all the words that have ch, sh, wh, and th sounds.

Cherie was a little chick. Cherie's mother was Shelly and her father was Thayer. Cherie had a little brother. He had white feathers. So everyone called him White.

One Thursday morning, White asked, 'Father, where are you taking us today?' Father Thayer said, 'Let's all go to the church.'

So Mother Shelly wore her best hat. Cherie and White wore their best shoes. Father pushed the wheelbarrow out of the shed. Soon all three sat and father pushed them down the lane. Cherie and White cheered. Mother Shelly said, 'Hush, children! Be quiet.'

Consonant Blend Bl

Read the words aloud. Can you hear the bl sound?

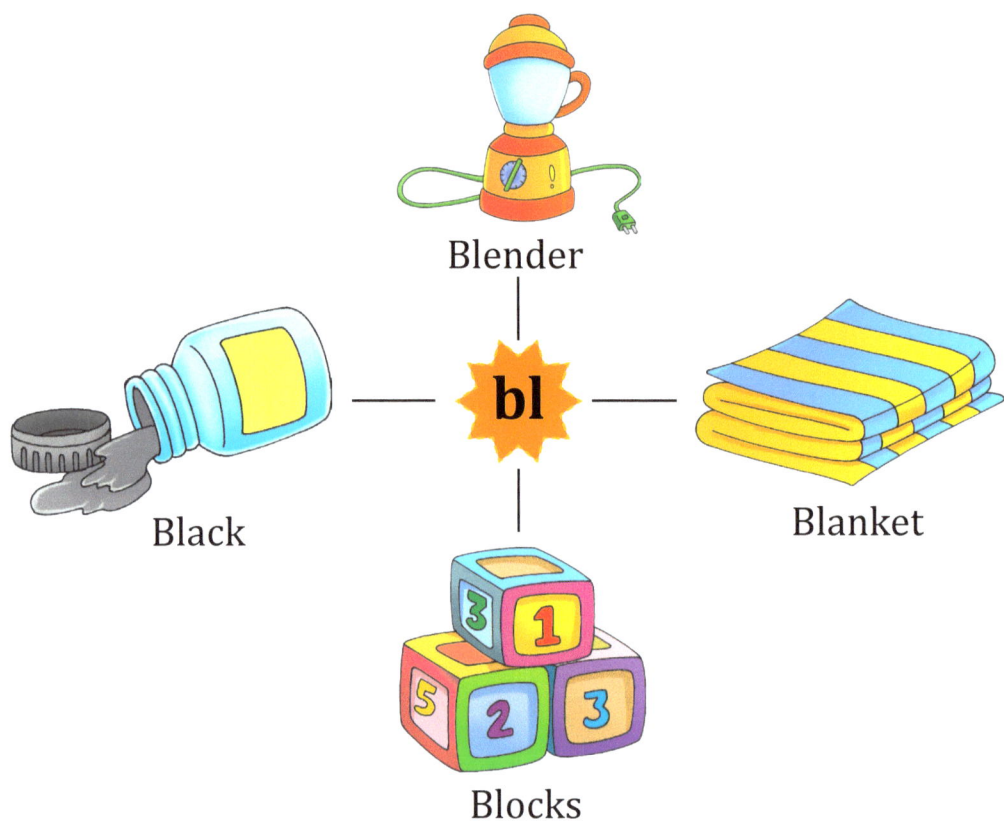

Read the poem and underline the bl words.

Two Little Birds

I saw a blackbird

Talking to a blue jay,

They talked about the blue sky

And the clouds that liked to fly.

They talked about the lambs that bleat

And the blueberries that they eat,

And when the wind blew over their heads

They said, 'Oh we are so blessed.'

Let's build words.

Bl
- ink ....
- ossom ....
- ue ....
- ow ....

Look, read and match.

Blister

Blueberry

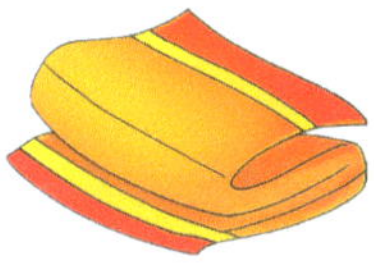

Blanket

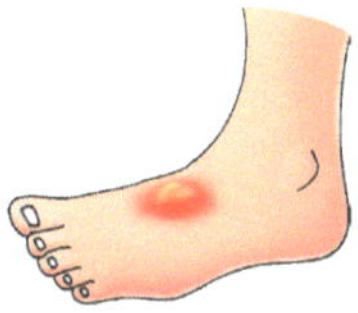

Blindfold

Blind

Consonant Blend Cl

Read the words aloud. Can you hear the cl sound?

Clock

Cliff

cl

Clap

Cloud

Read the poem and circle the cl words.

The Little Cloud

The little cloud was lost
It had no clue where to go,
It climbed over the hills
And looked down on the mills.
It floated above the clear seas
And talked to the breeze.
At last the little cloud
Reached a cliff,
And rained down in a jiff.

Teaching Tips:
Play a game of charades with the students. Tell them to act out active words starting with cl and tell the others to guess. For example, clean, climb, claw, etc.

38

Write three new words with cl.

....

Write the correct words in these boxes.

| Click | Club | Clue | Class |

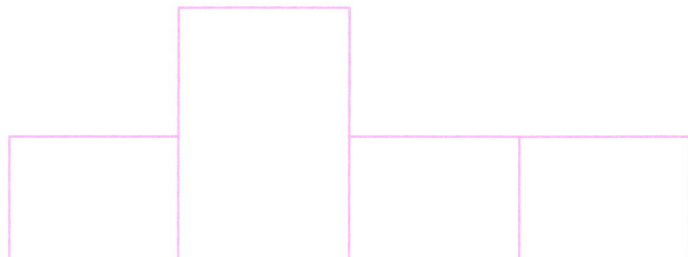

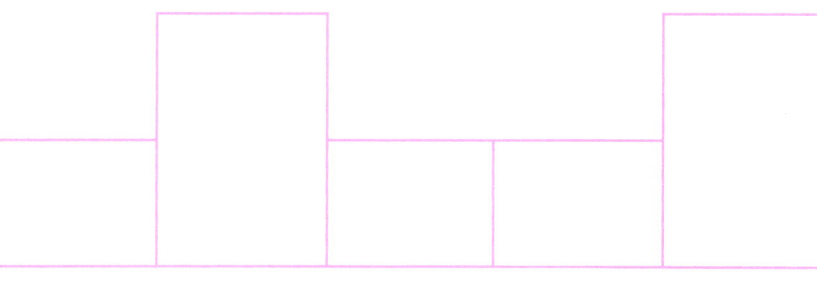

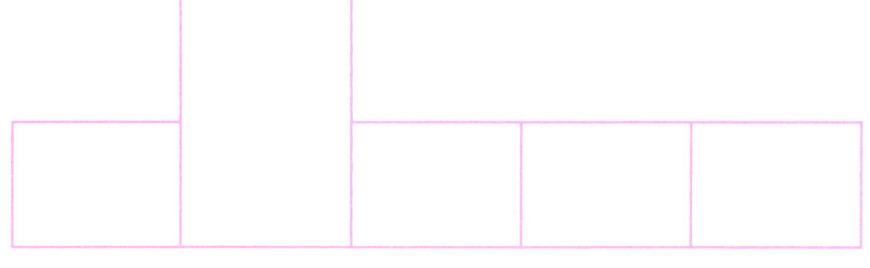

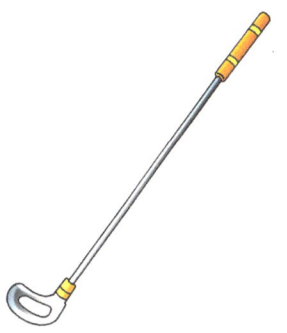
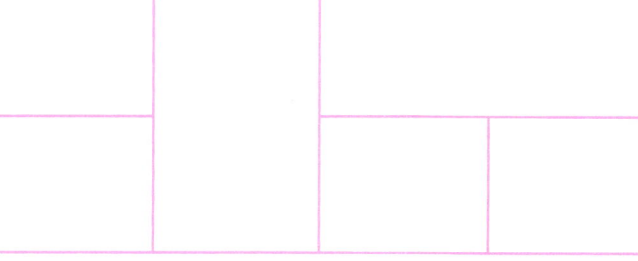

Consonant Blend Fl

Read the words aloud. Can you hear the fl sound?

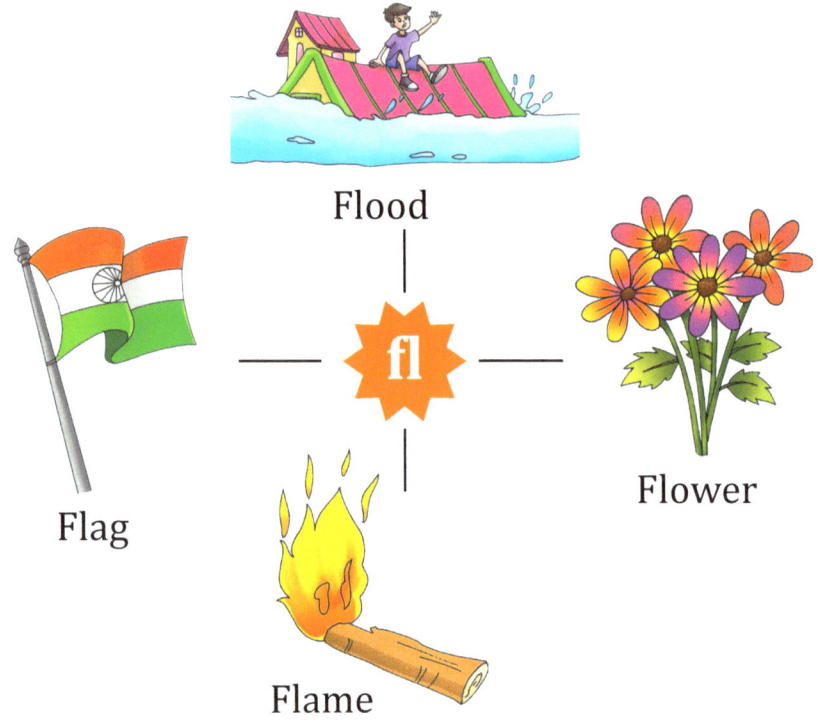

Read the poem and circle the fl words.

The Flea

I saw a flea

When it saw me

It began to flee.

It crawled on the floor,

And reached the door,

It ran over my flip flops,

And jumped on my book,

I closed the flap,

But the flea flew away in a flash.

Let's build words.

Fl
- ag ....
- ower ....
- oat ....
- ipper ....

Find the following words in the word search below.

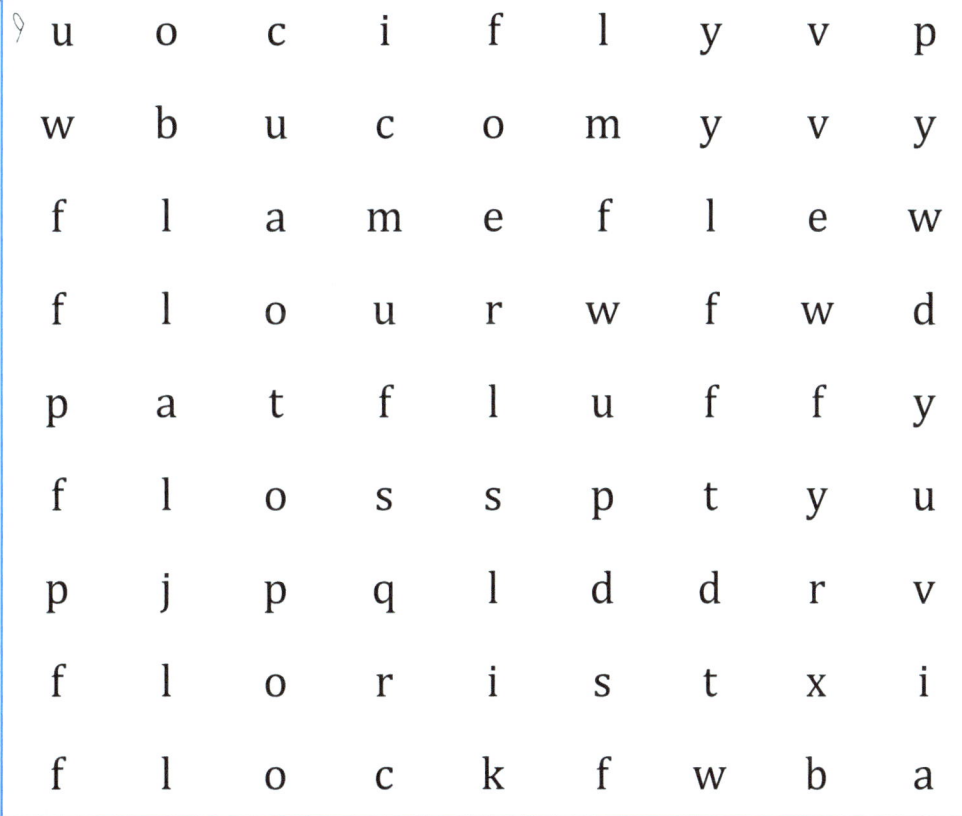

| fly |
| florist |
| fluffy |
| floss |
| flour |
| flock |
| flew |
| flame |

Consonant Blend Gl

Read the words aloud. Can you hear the gl sound?

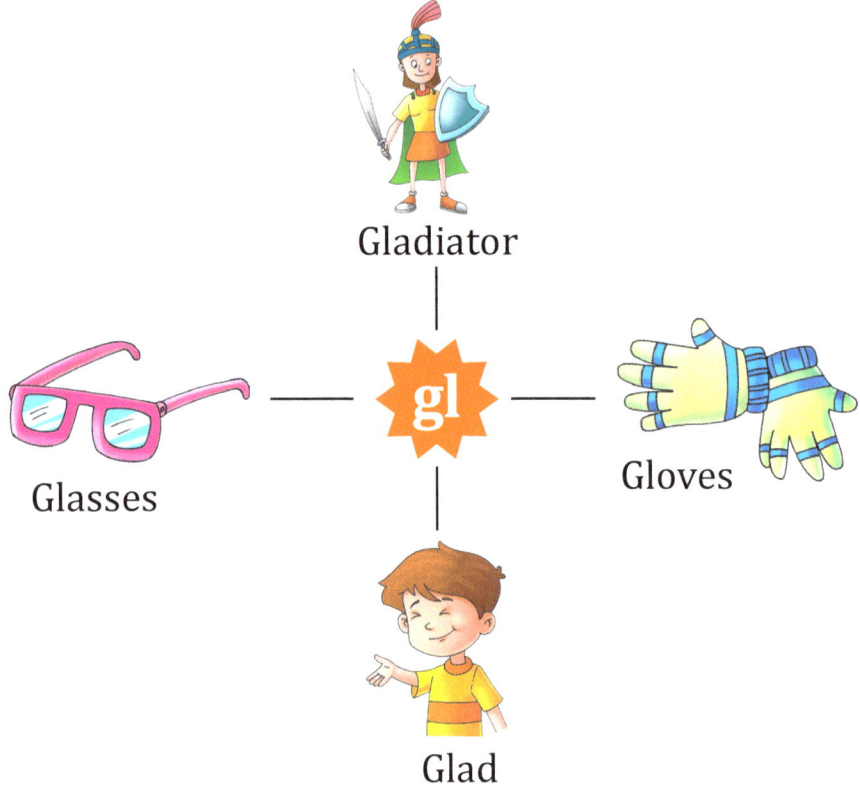

Look at the pictures and say the names. Cross out the objects that do not begin with the gl sound. Write the names of the objects that begin with the gl sound.

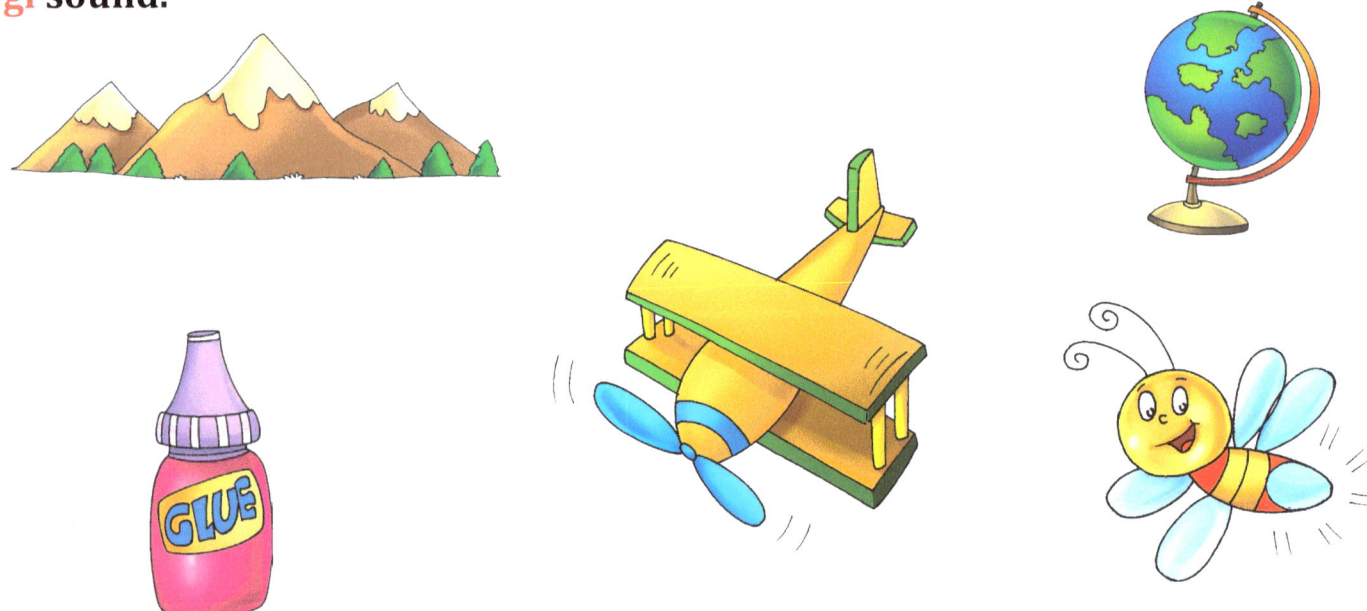

Read the story. Circle all the words that begin with gl.

Glen and Glenda were very glad. They were going to see a glacier. 'Wear your gloves. It is going to be very cold.'

They sat in a cable car. It took them to the glacier. The glacier was a river of ice. It looked glassy and white. It glittered in the sunlight. 'It is the most beautiful thing we have ever seen,' Glen and Glenda said with glee.

Consonant Blend Pl

Look at the pictures and write the words. Cross out the ones that do not begin with the pl sound.

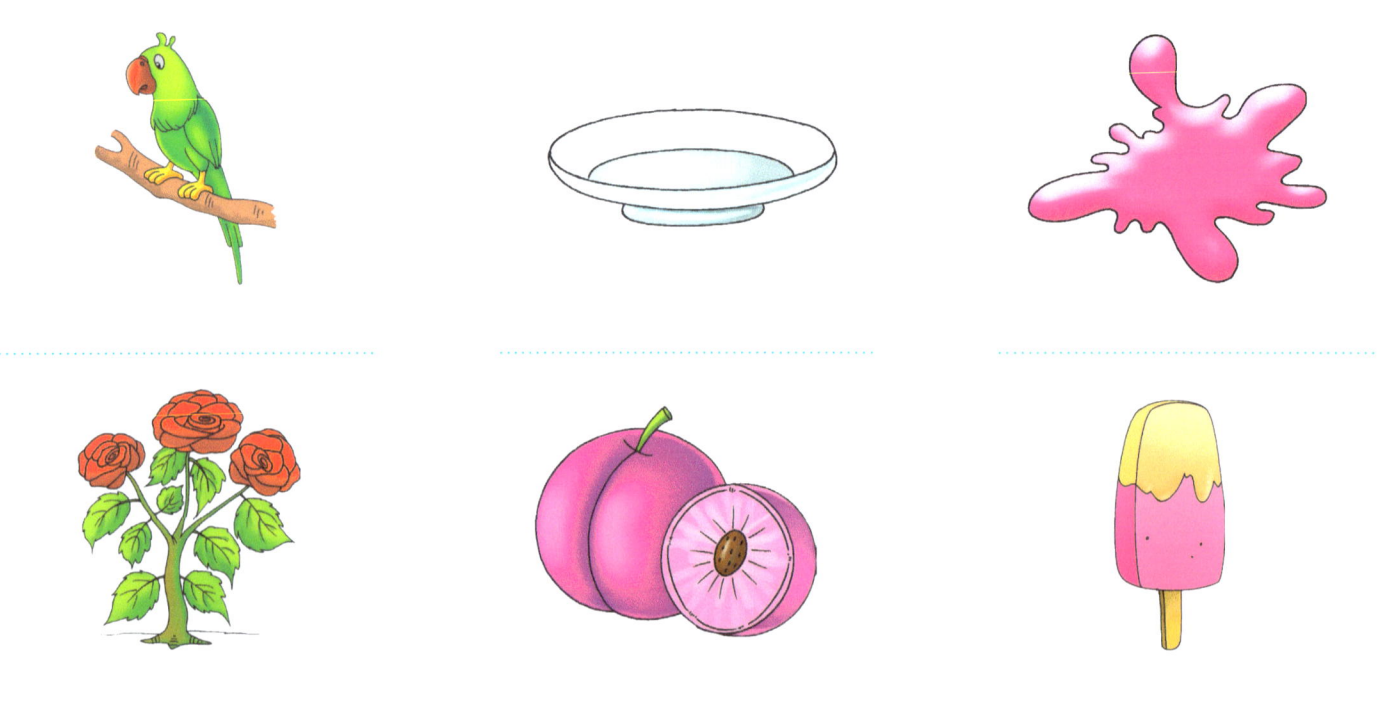

Unscramble the words.

lusp: It is the opposite of minus. ....

lumpbre: He repairs taps and pipes. ....

umlp: A small purple fruit. ....

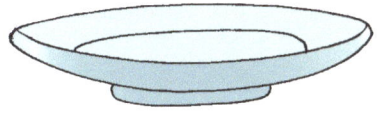

letap: We serve food on it. ....

Read the poem and underline all the pl words in it.

Plato

Plato the platypus,

Lives in a zoo,

Along with a gnu.

Plato likes to play,

All night and day.

He likes to eat plants and plums,

Which he shares with his mum.

Learn More

Fill in the blanks with the correct consonant blend.

| Fr | Bl | Cr | Cl | Sc | Pl | Gr | Fl | Dr | Gl | Br |

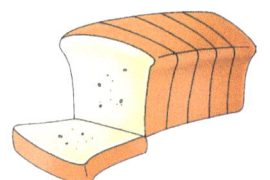 ....ead

 ....oud

 ....y

 ....ant

 ....ock

 ....ue

 ....ab

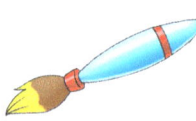 ....ush

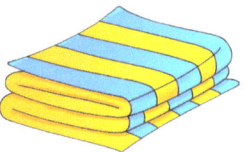 ....anket

 ....apes

 ....um

 ....og

Short or Long Vowel?

Look at the picture and circle the correct word. Copy the correct word in the space given.

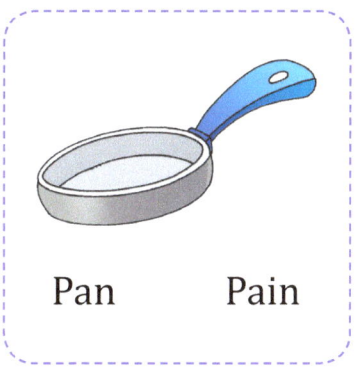
Pan   Pain

Cot   Coat

Ran   Rain

Fin   Fine

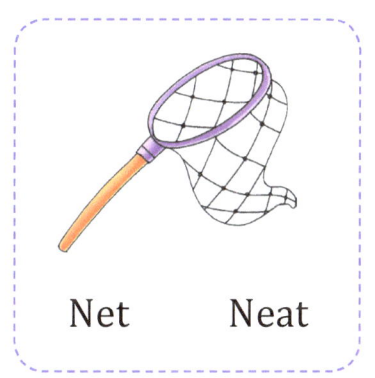
Net   Neat

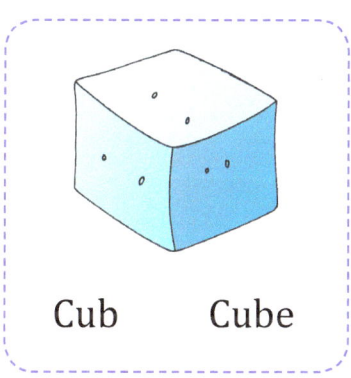
Cub   Cube

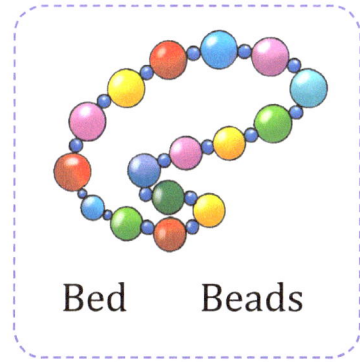
Bed   Beads

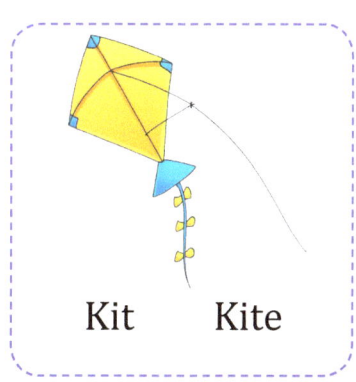
Kit   Kite

Long Vowel A

Read these words. Can you hear the long vowel a sound?

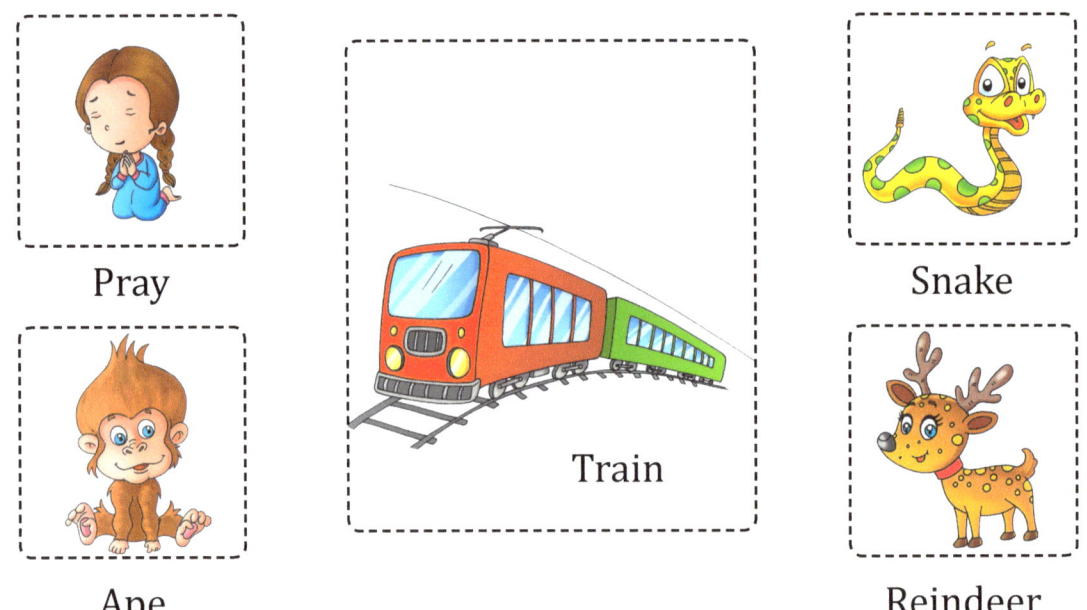

Pray

Ape

Train

Snake

Reindeer

Say the name of each picture. Circle the ones that have a long vowel a sound in them.

Teaching Tips:

There are four main ways to spell long vowel a sound: ae as in whale, ay as in play, ai as in snail and ei as in reindeer.

www.ingramcontent.com/pod-product-compliance
Lightning Source LLC
Chambersburg PA
CBHW040056160426
43192CB00002B/89